I03395494

A SPECIAL REQUEST PLEASE

A simple review on Amazon really helps us out! If you could take some time to leave one, you are awesome!

1

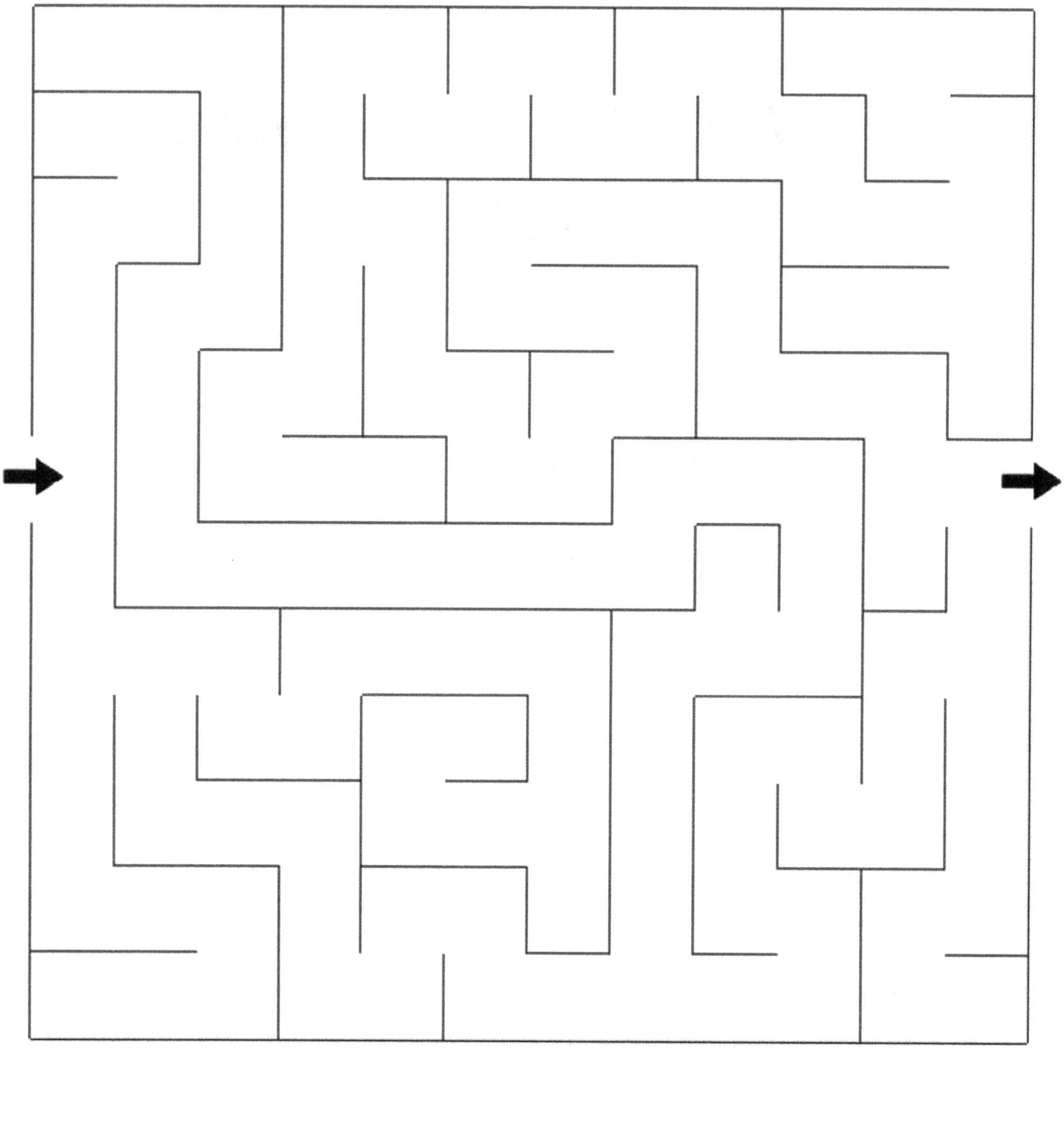

2

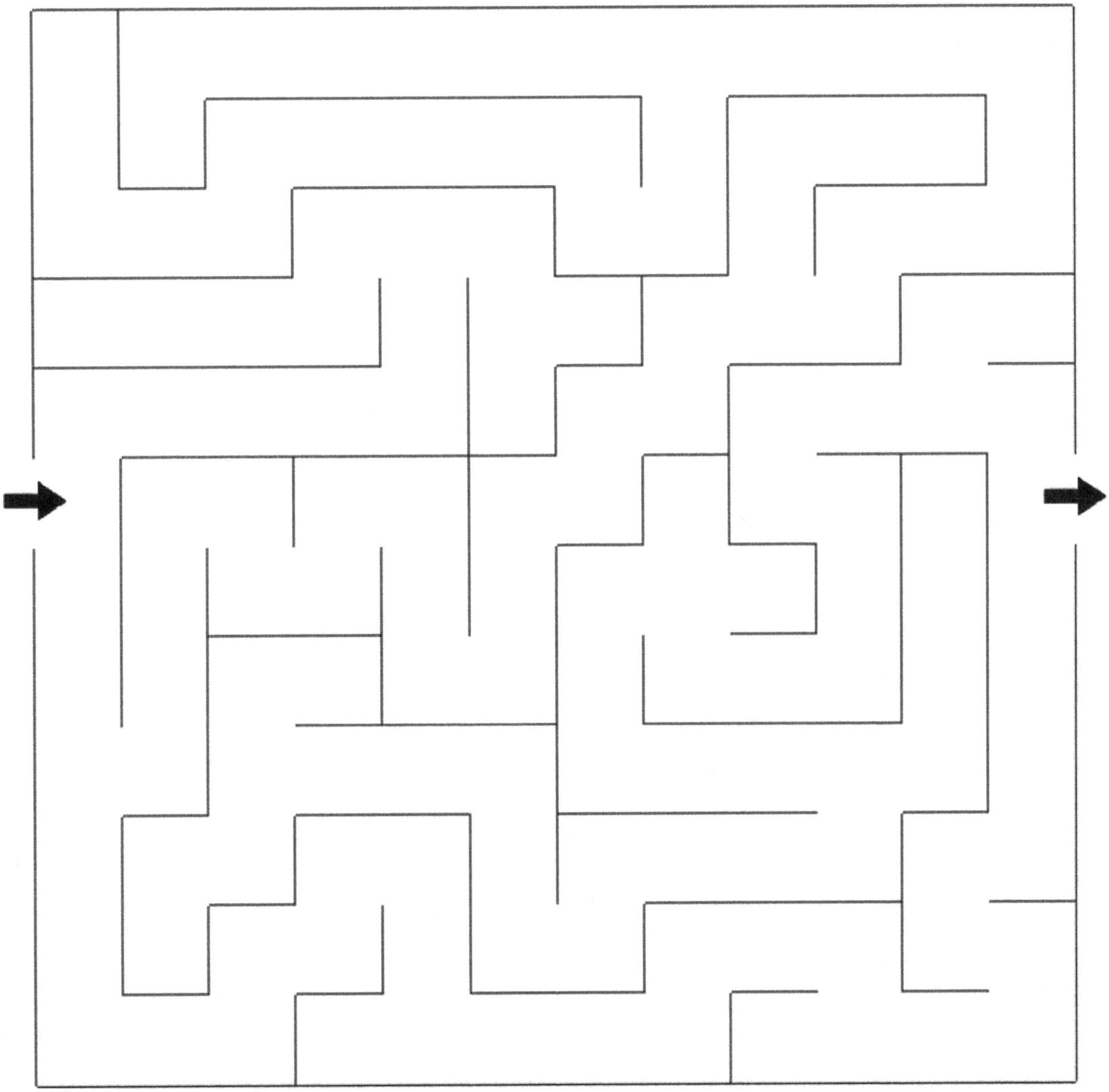

3

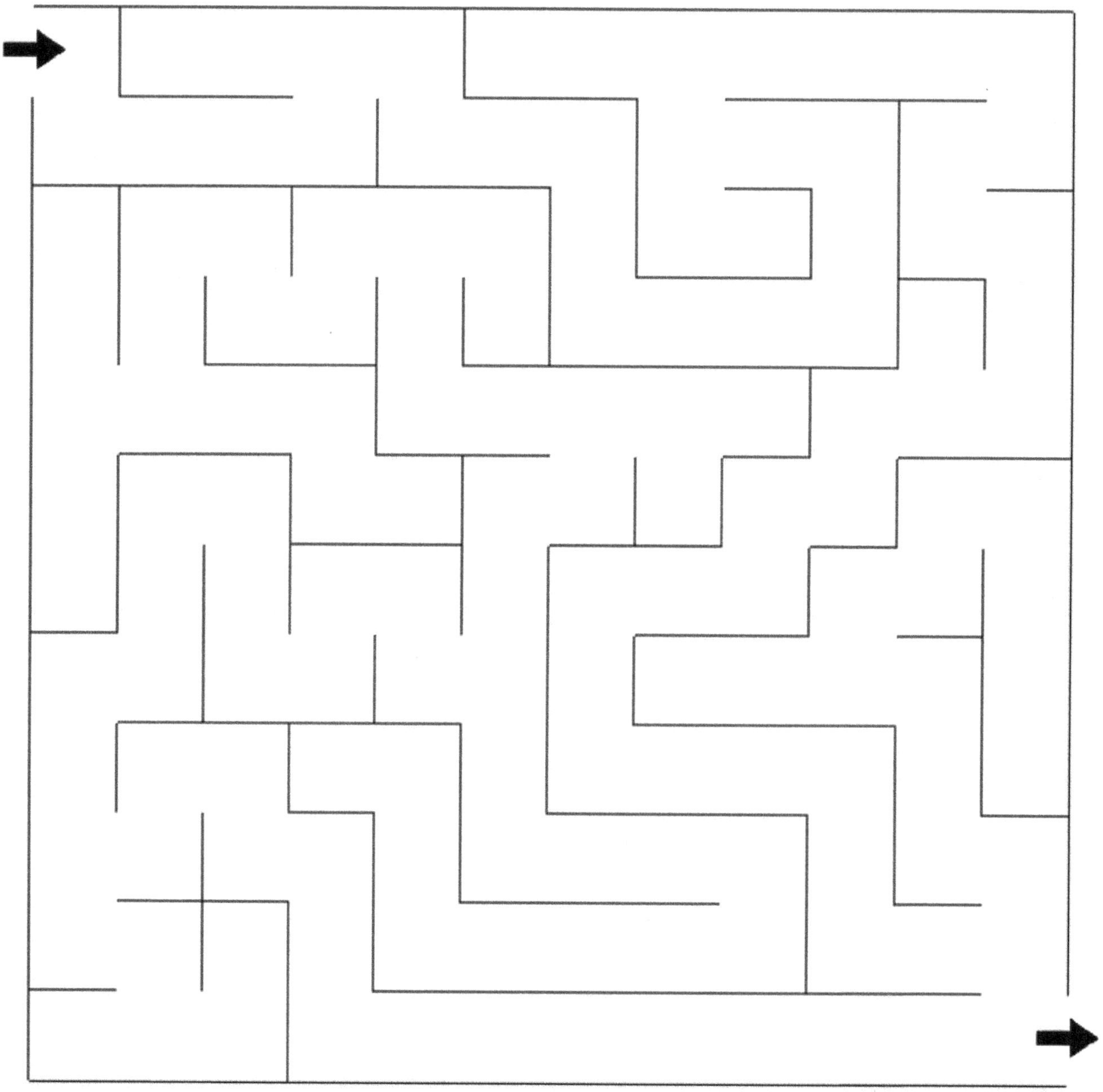

4

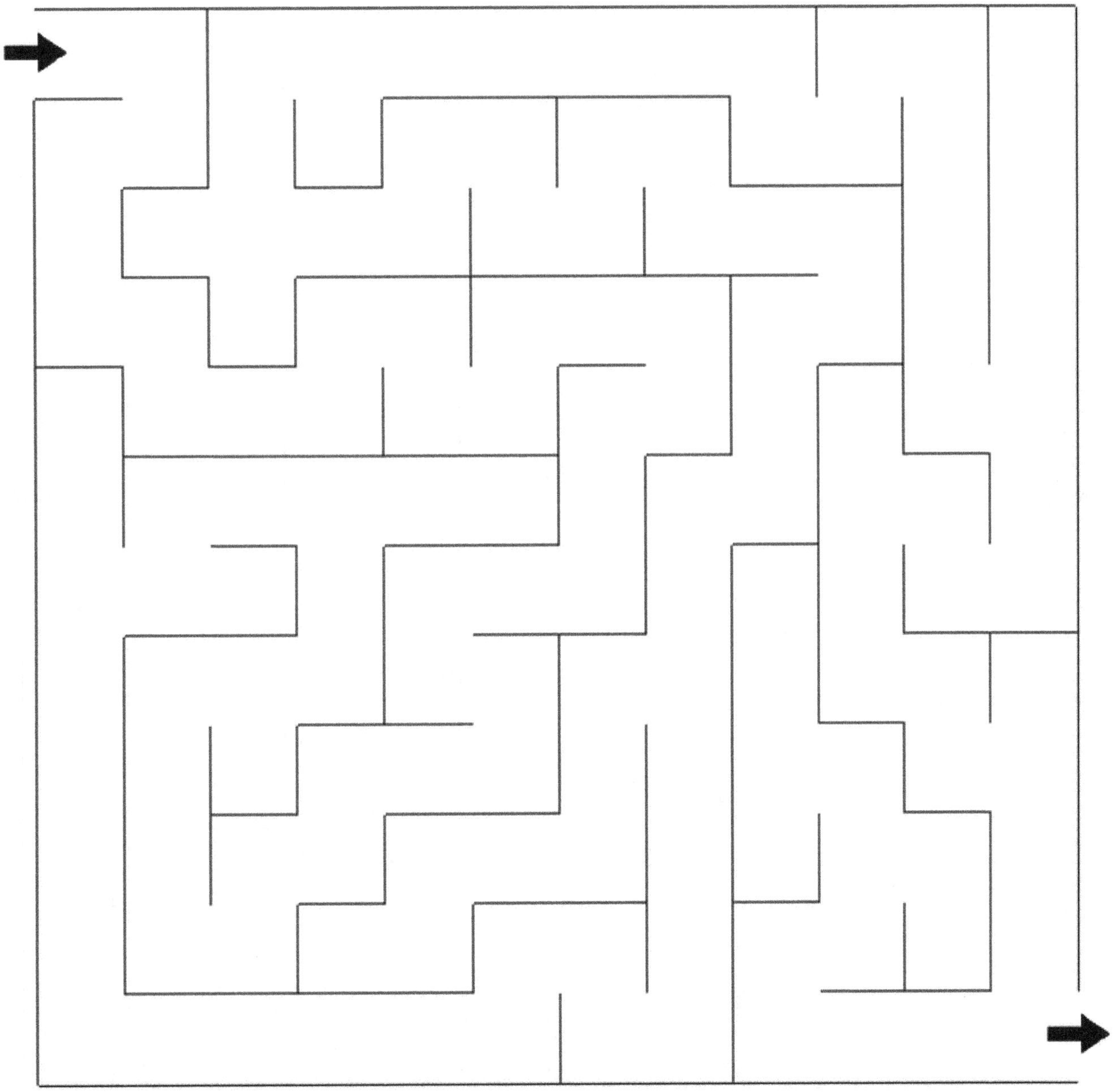

5

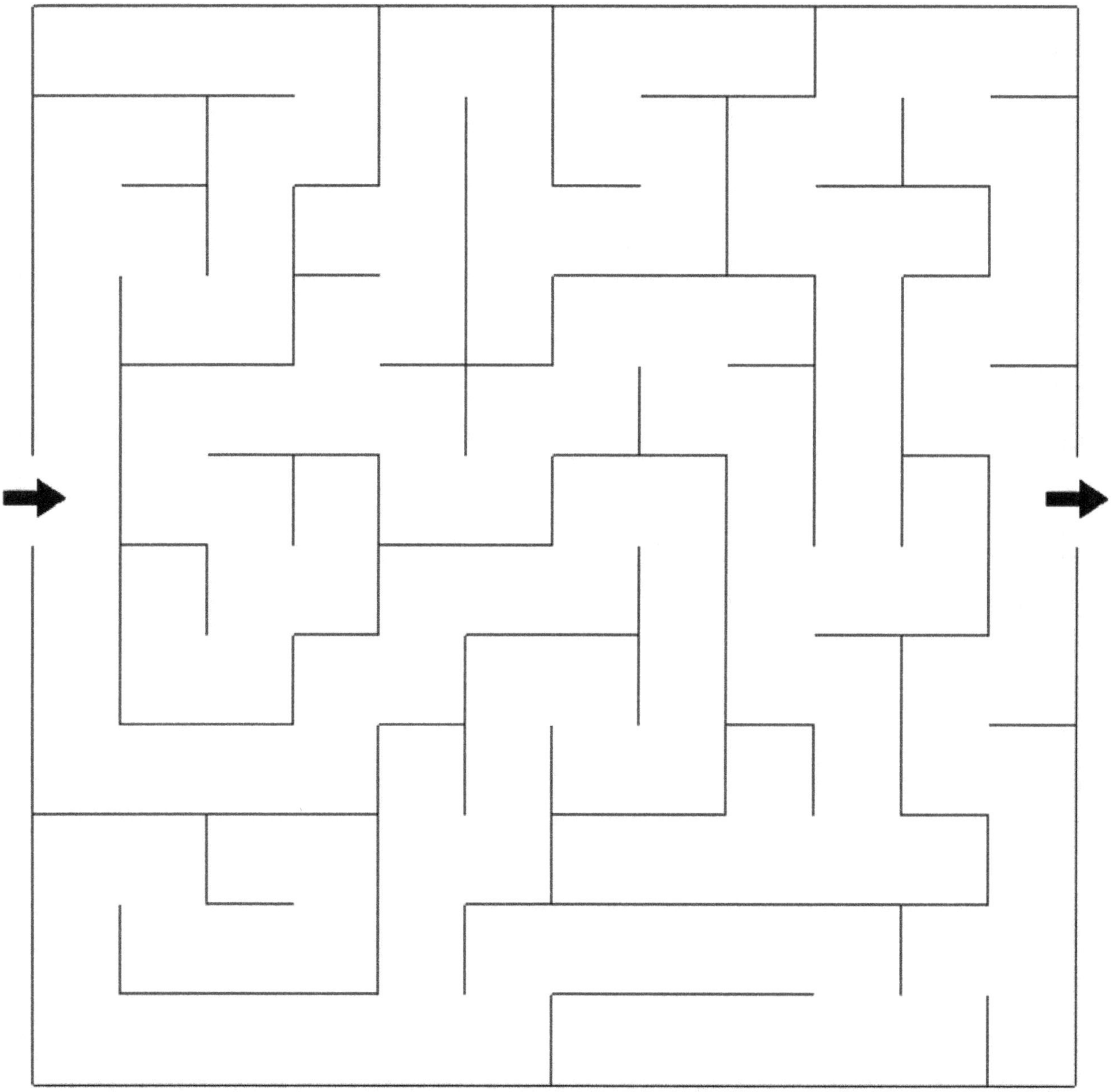

6

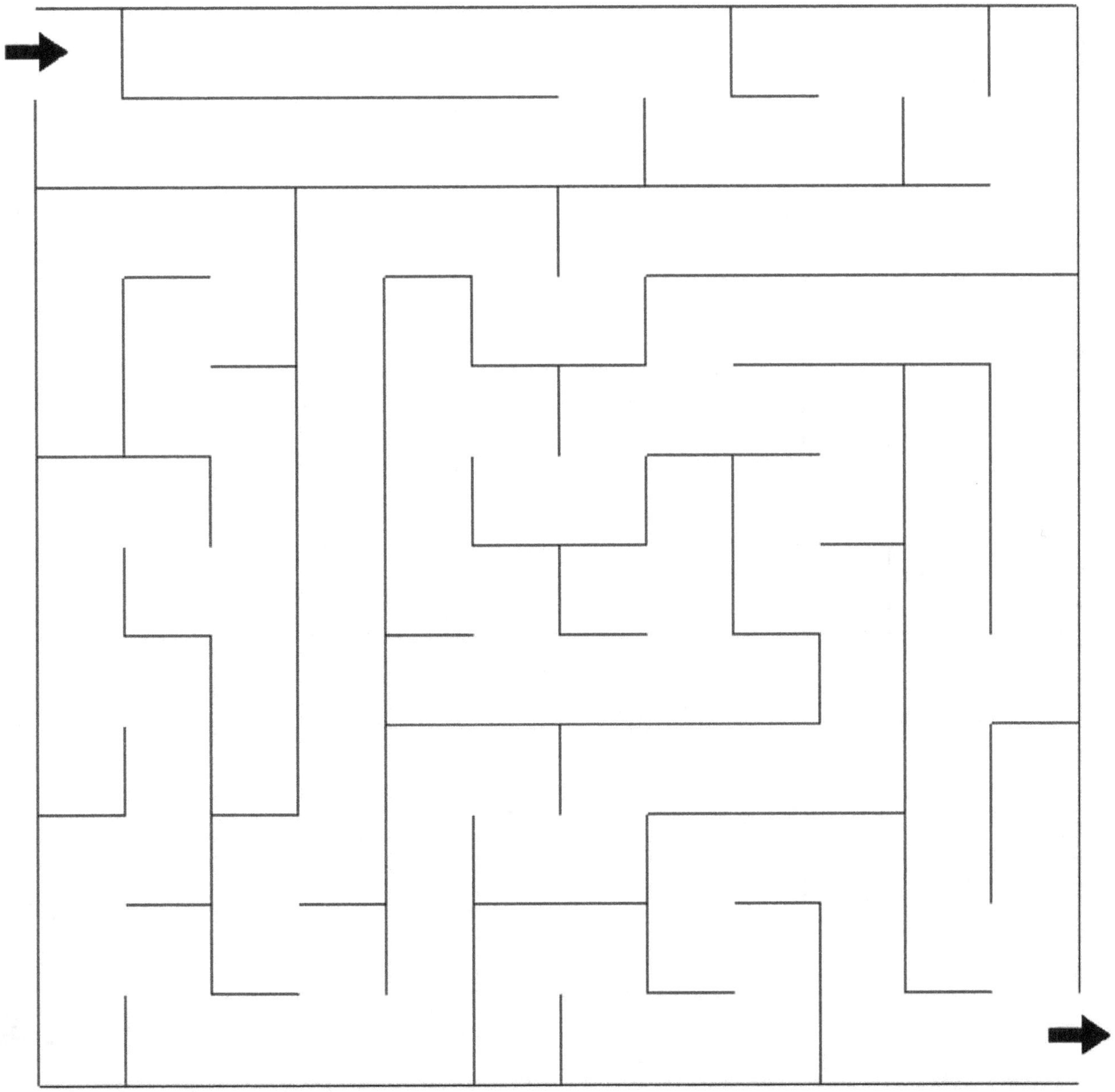

7

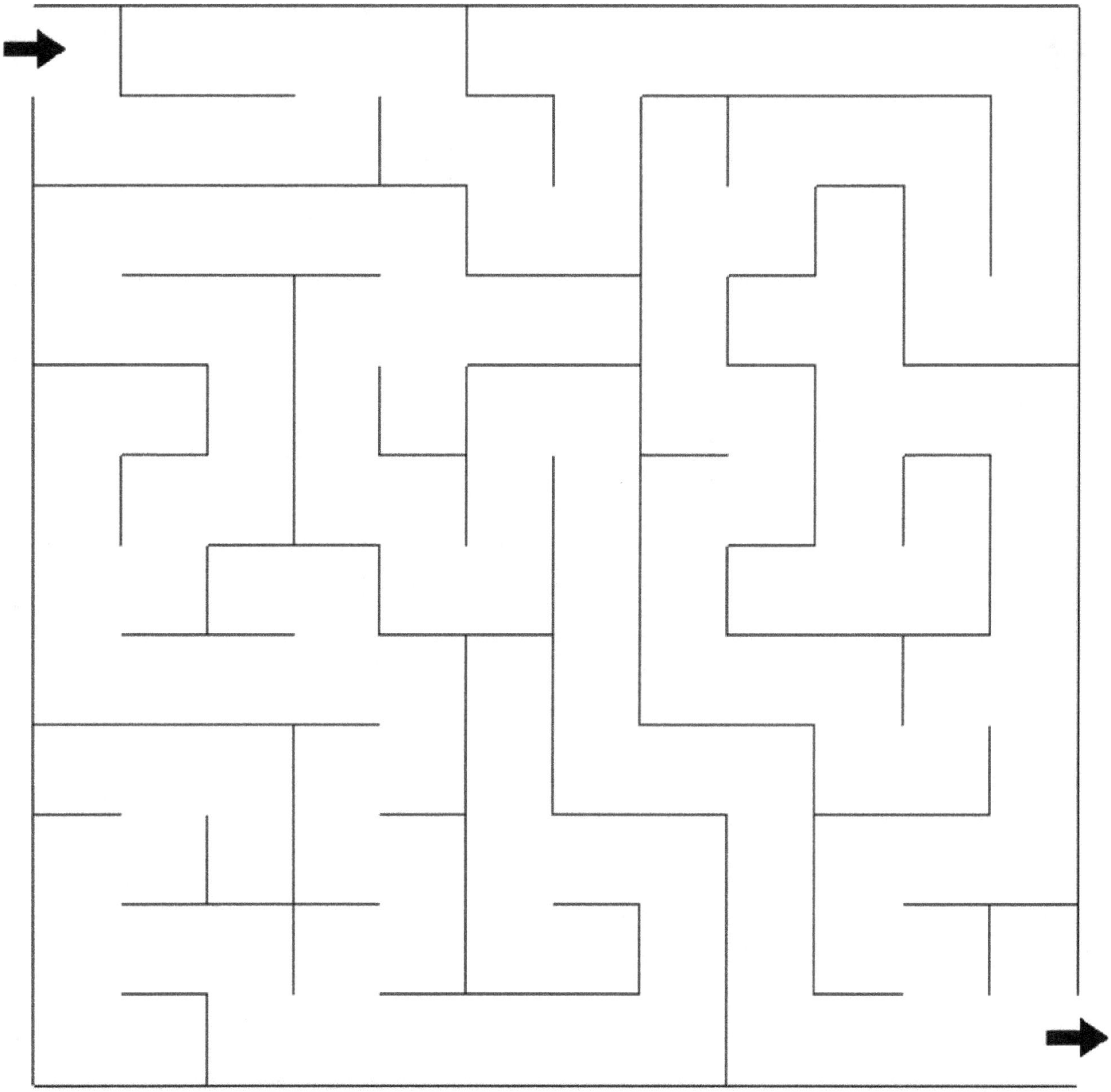

8

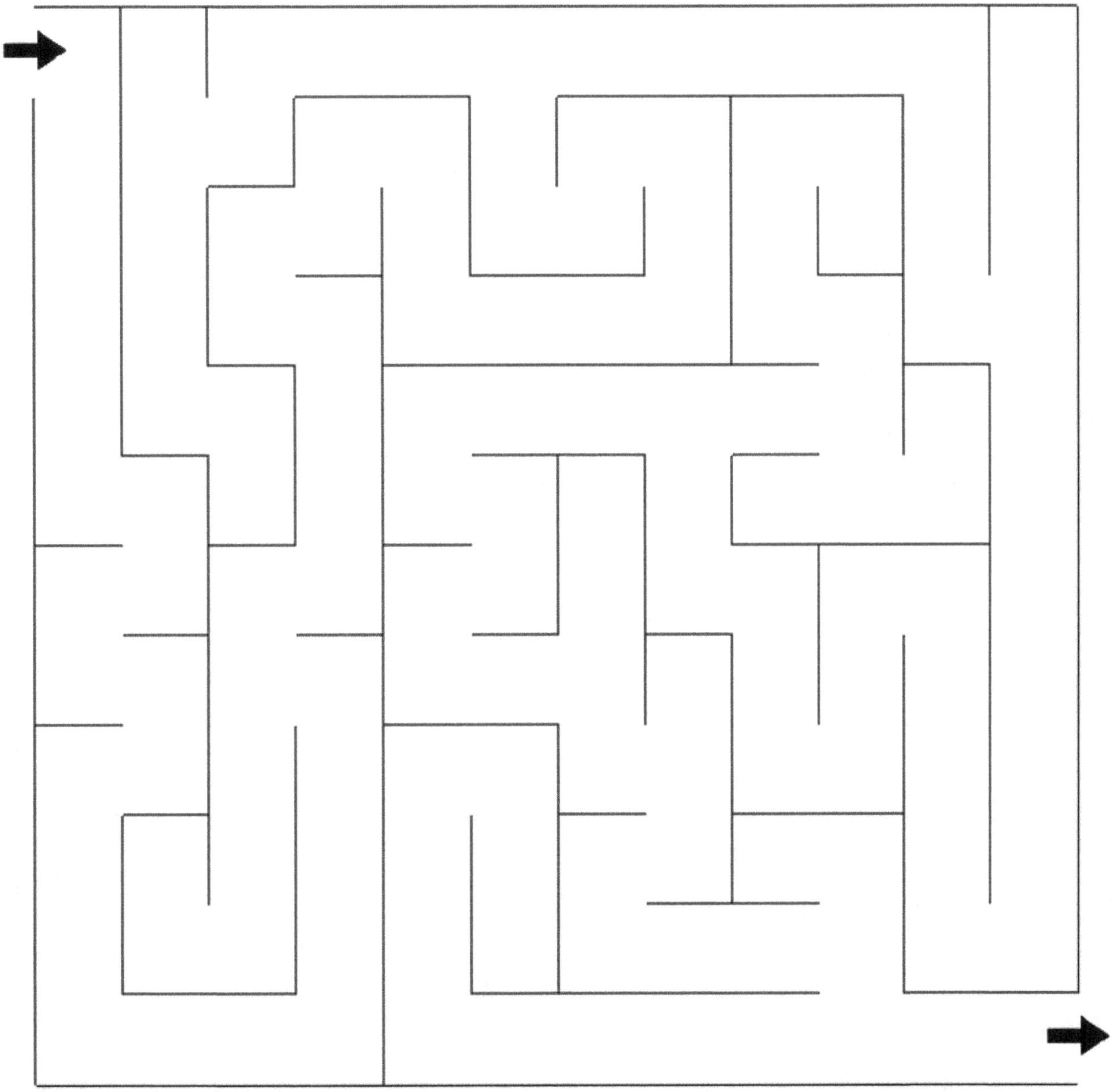

9

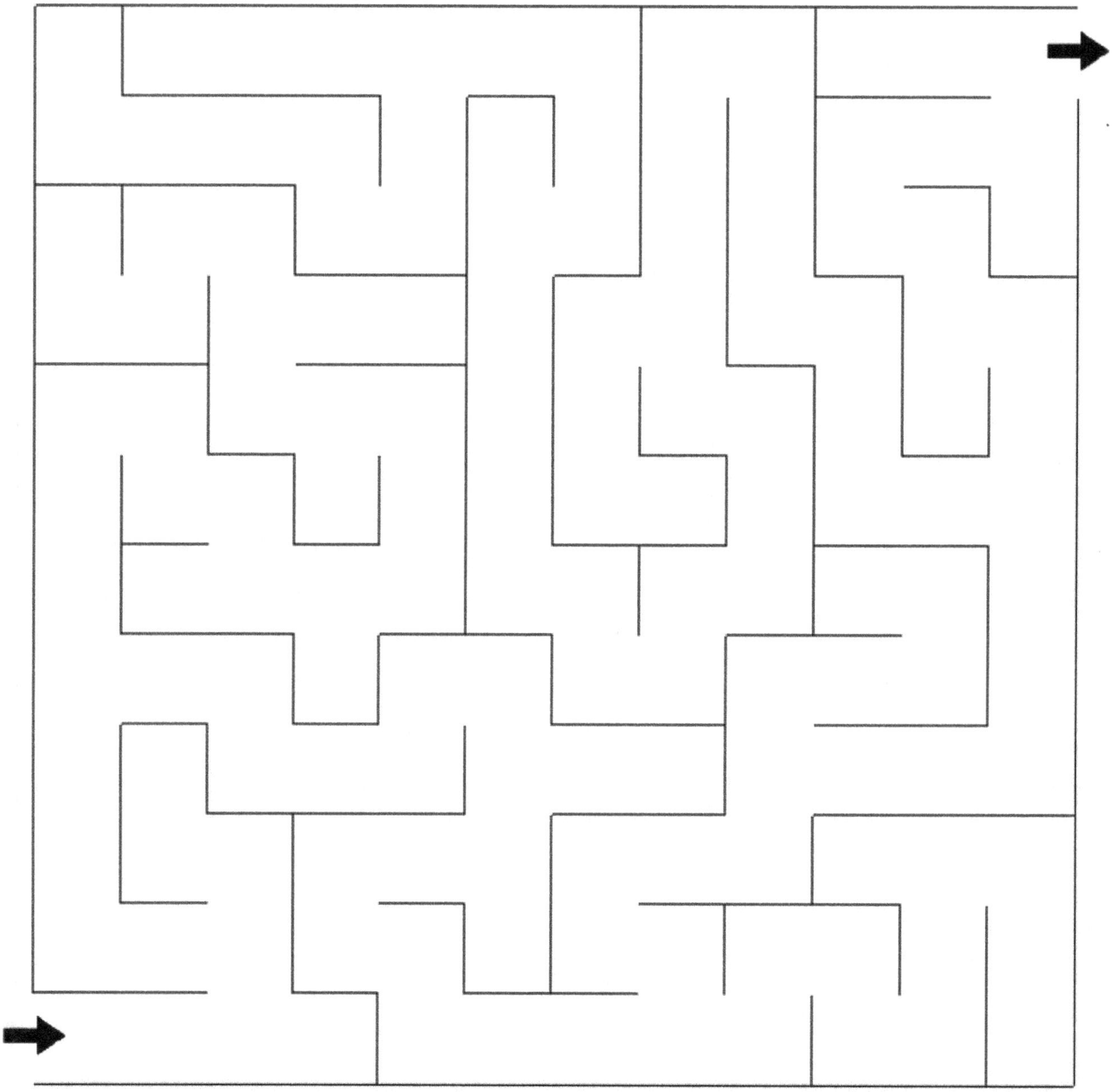

10

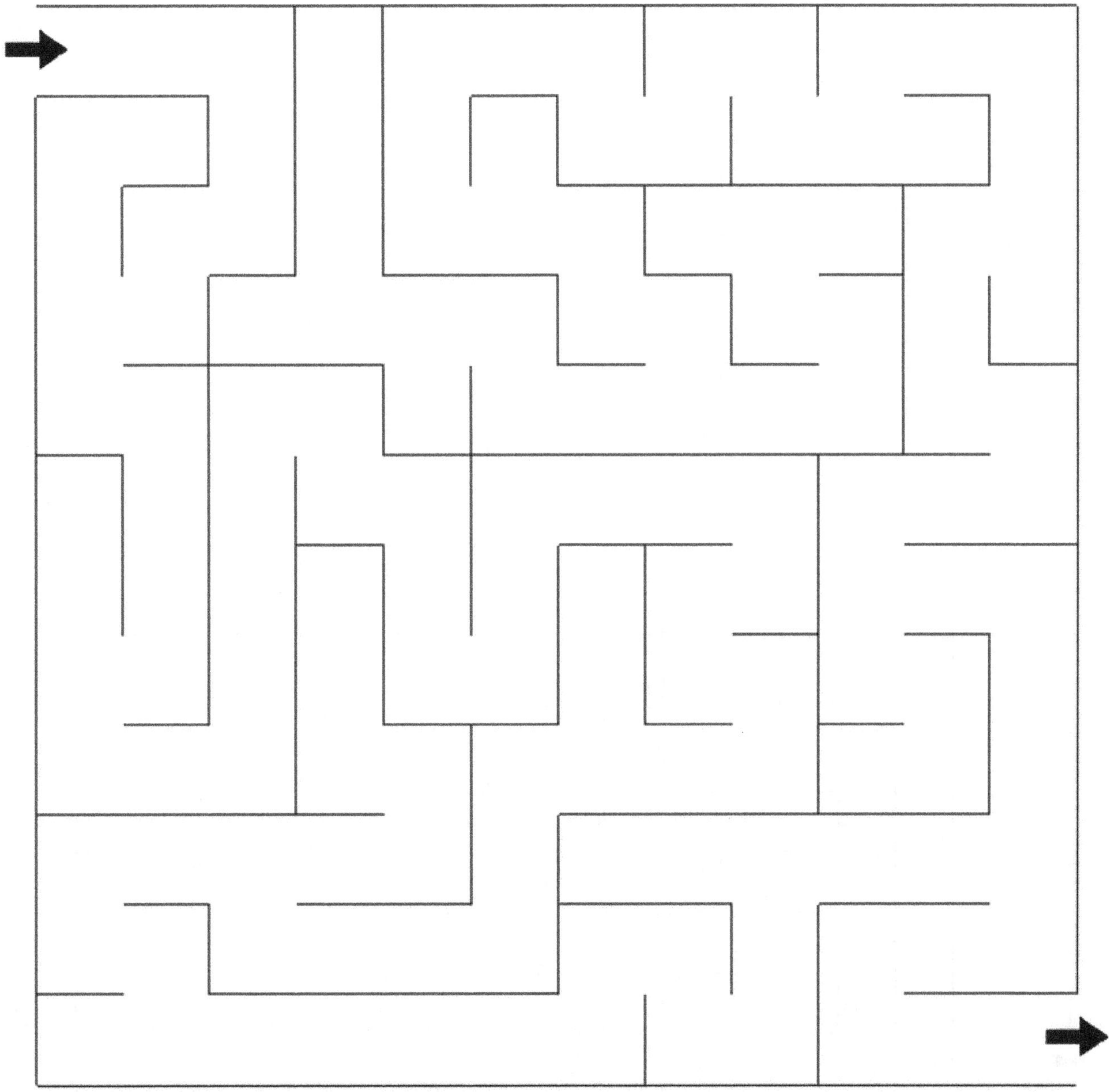

11

12

13

14

15

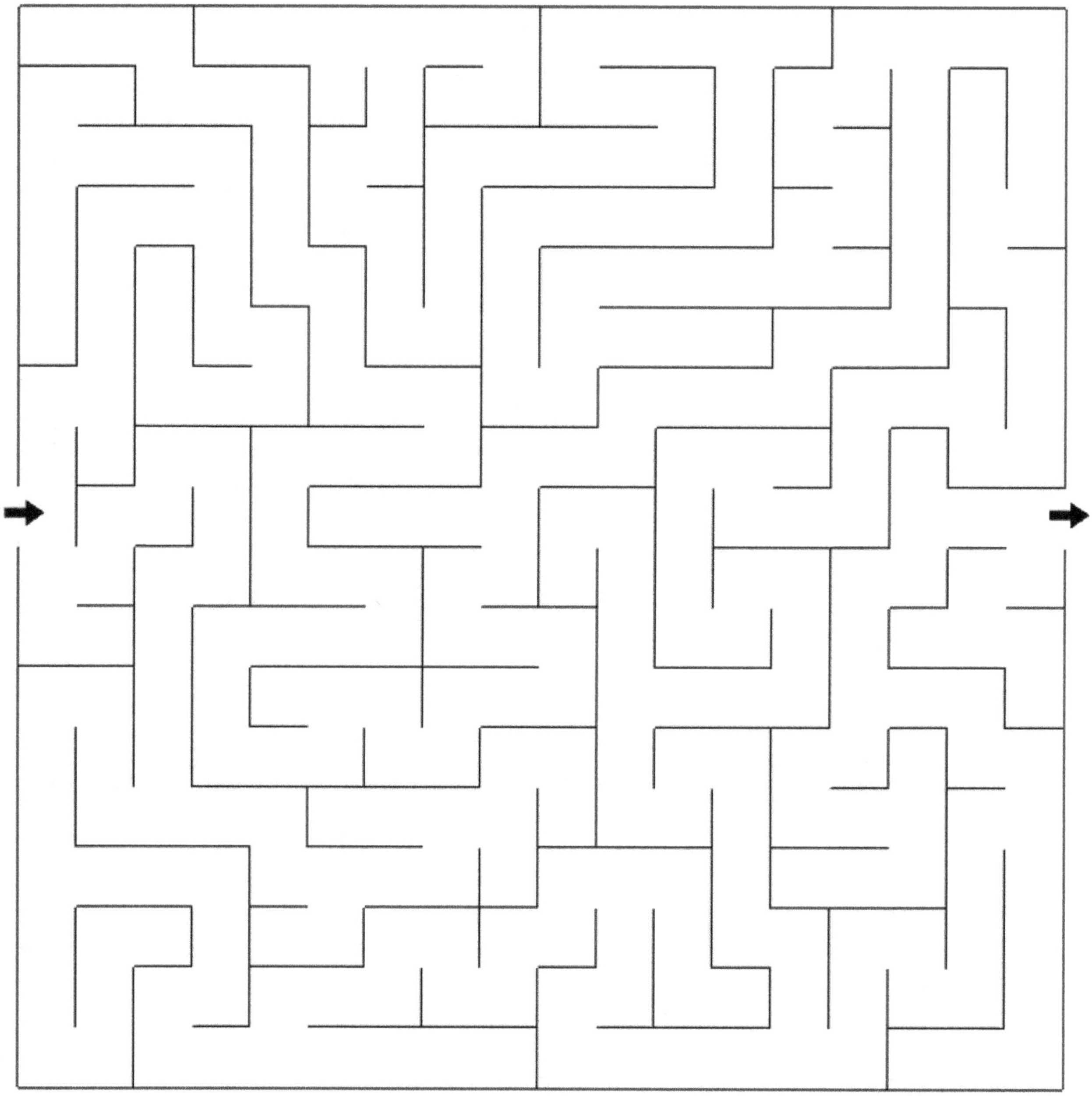

16

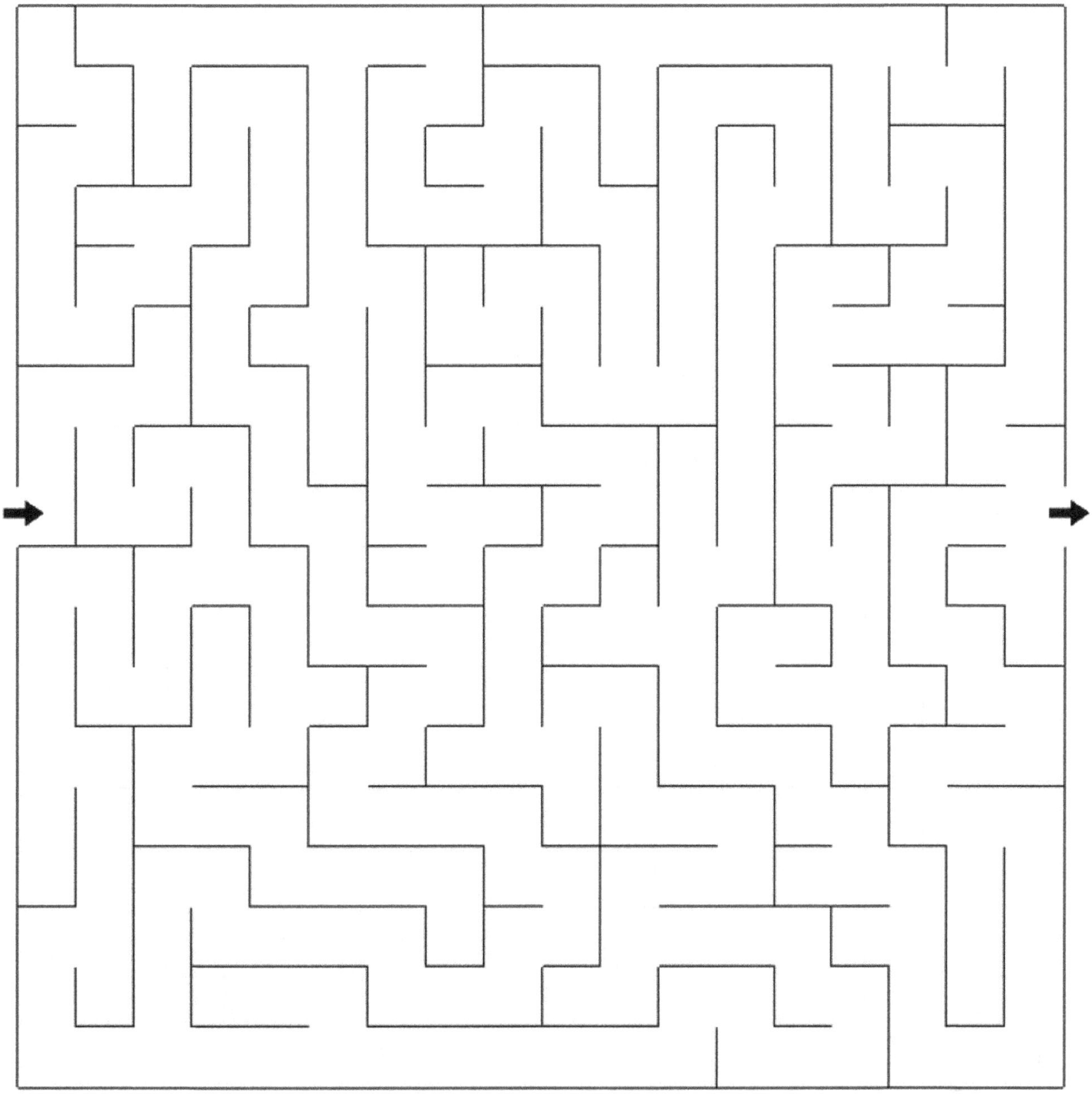

17

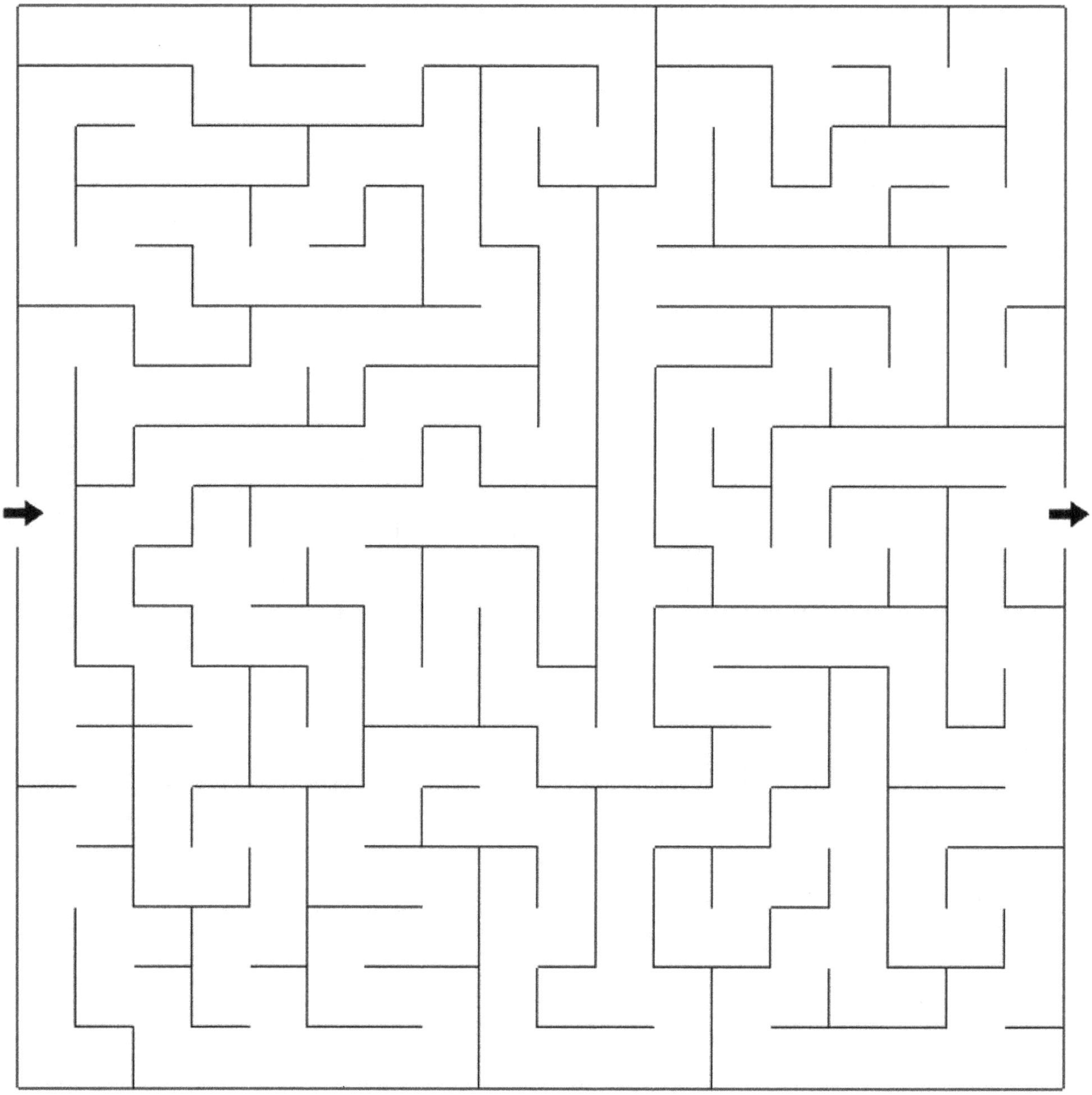

18

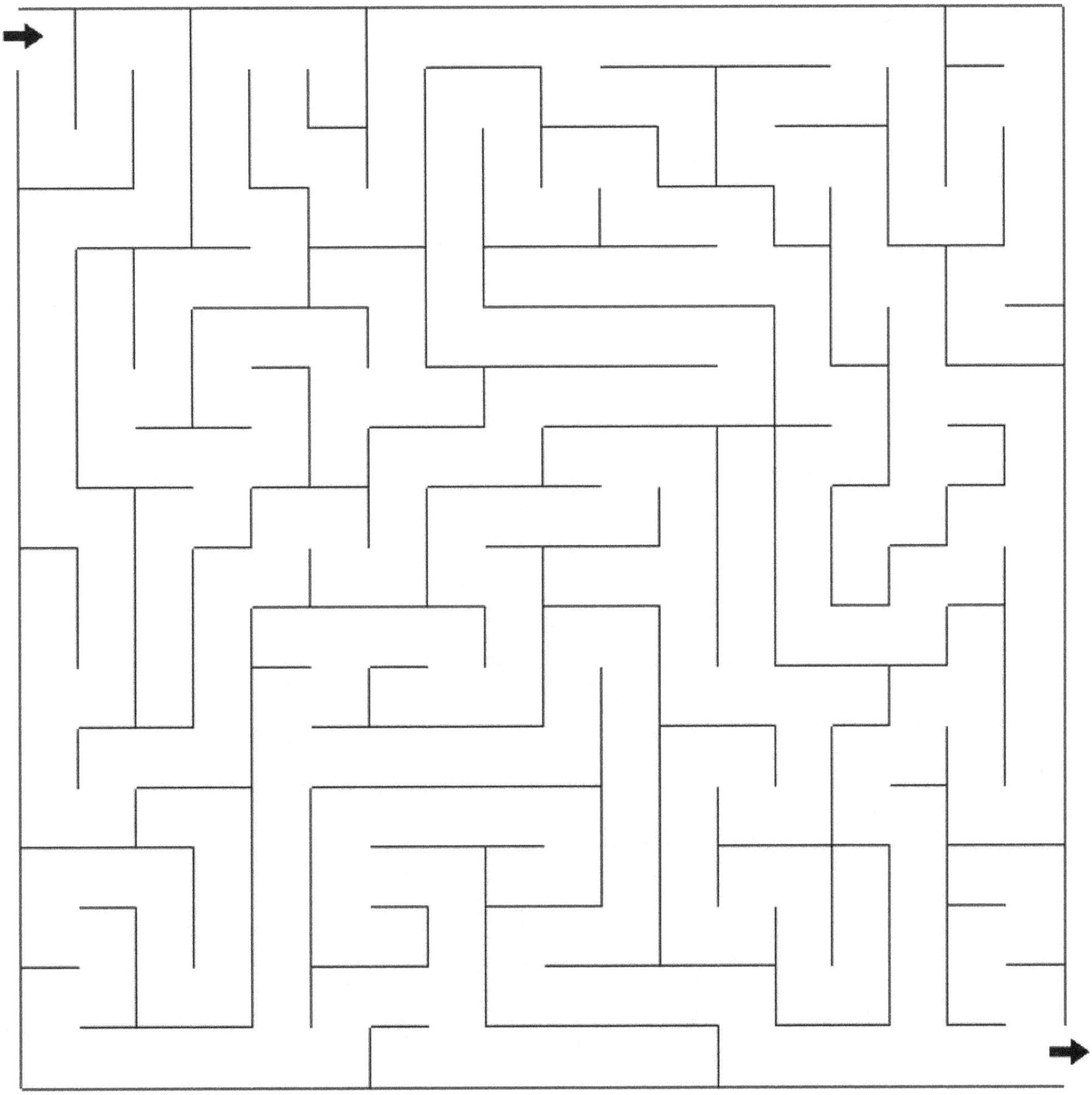

19

20

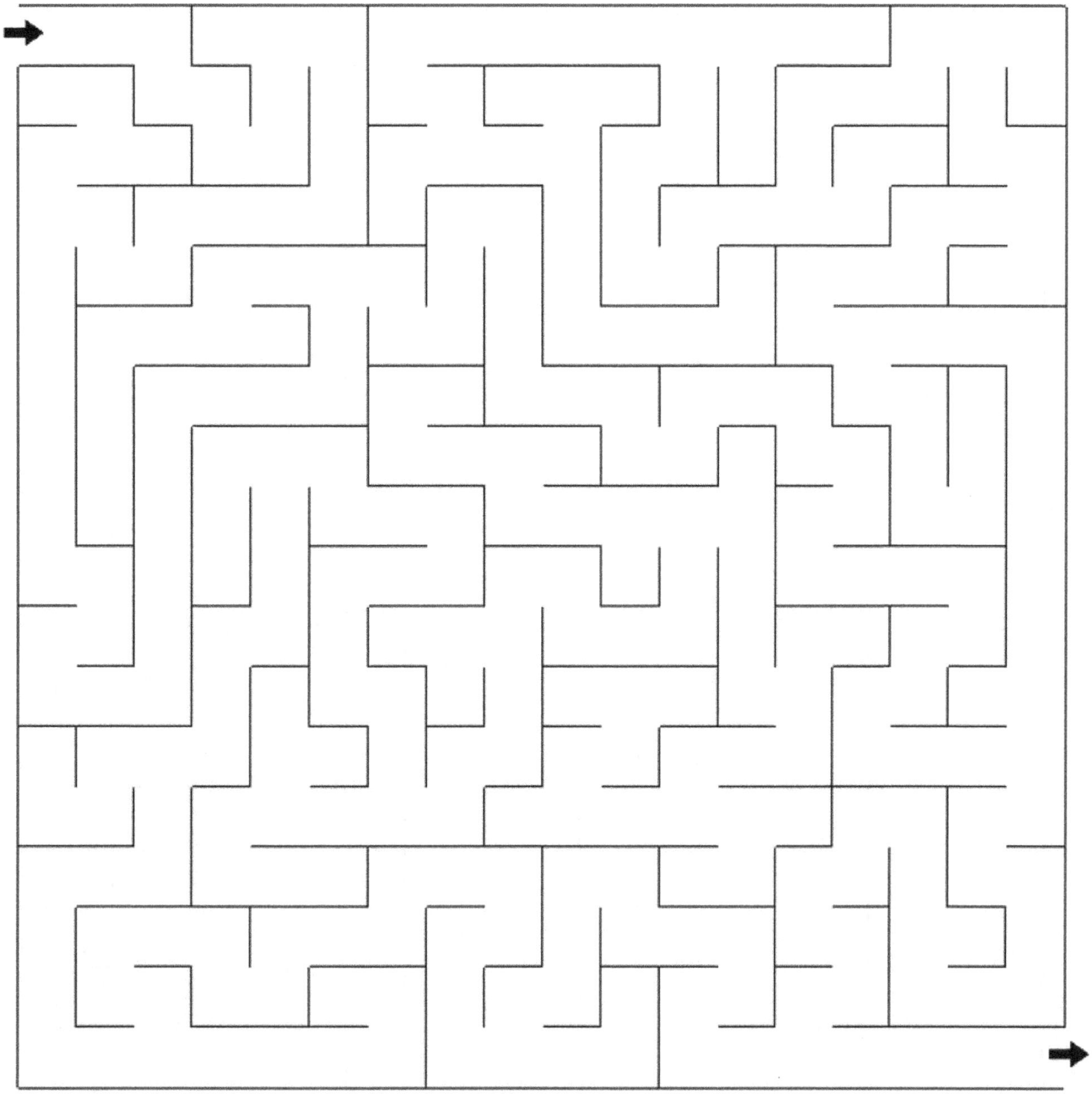

21

22

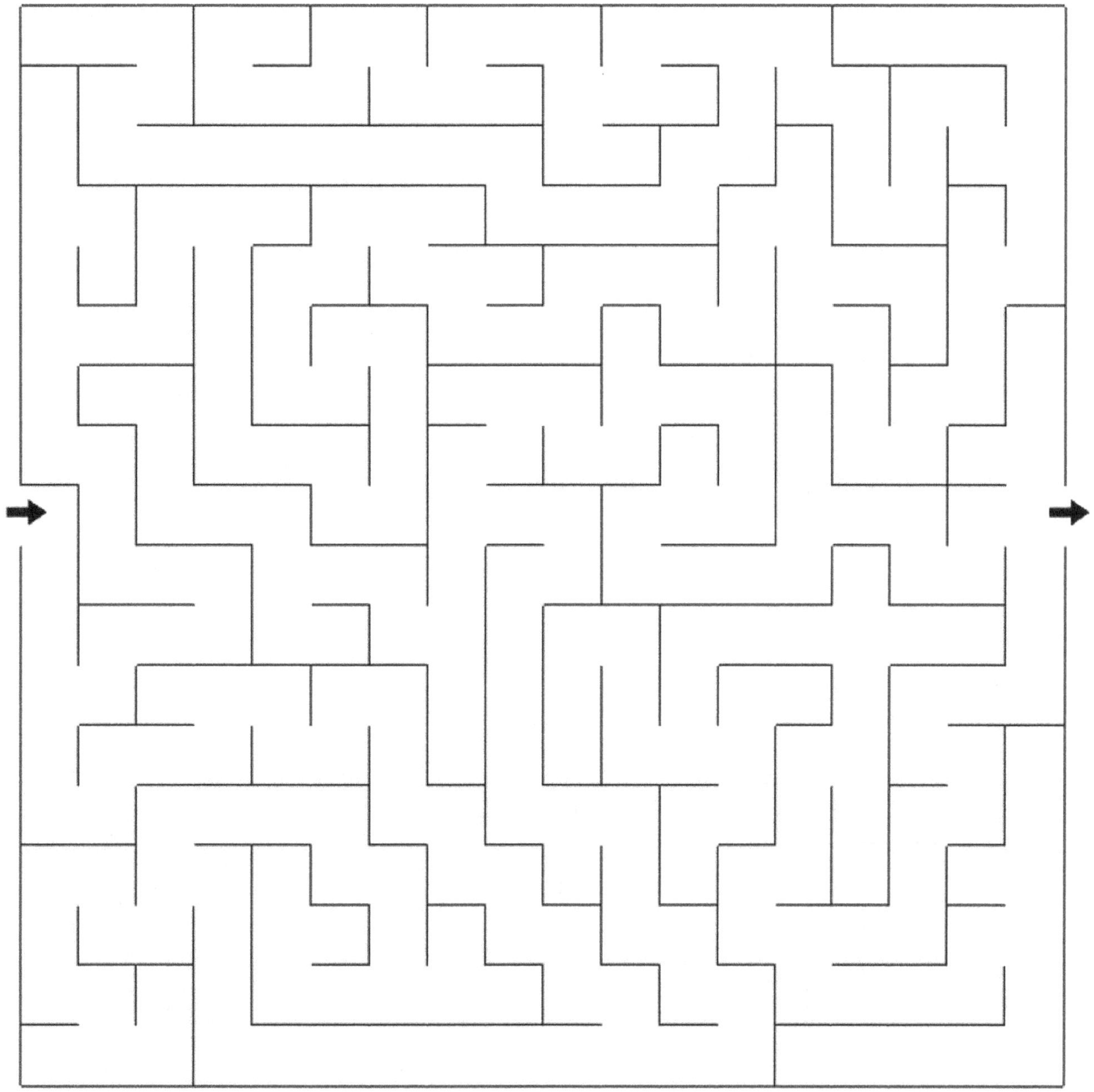

23

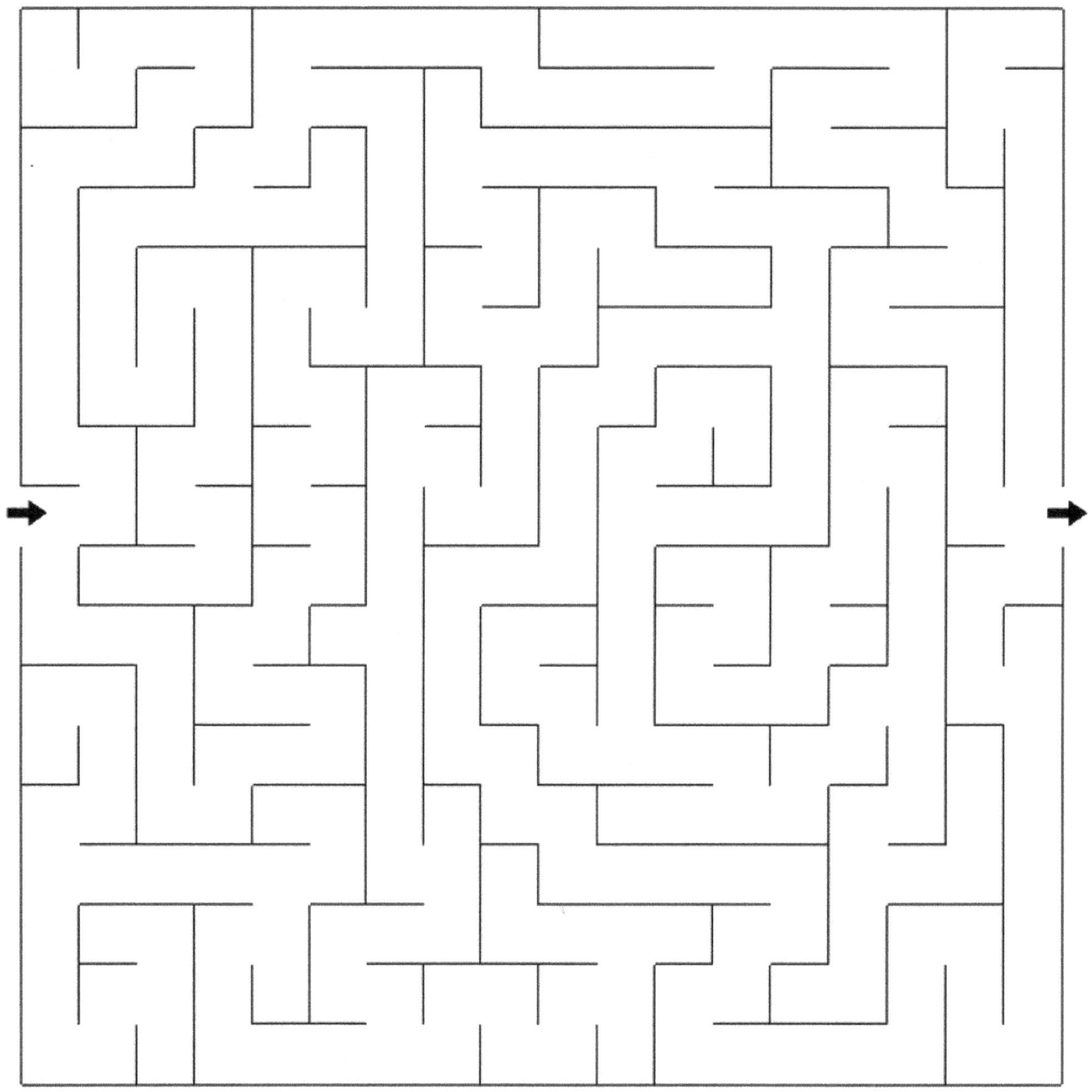

24

25

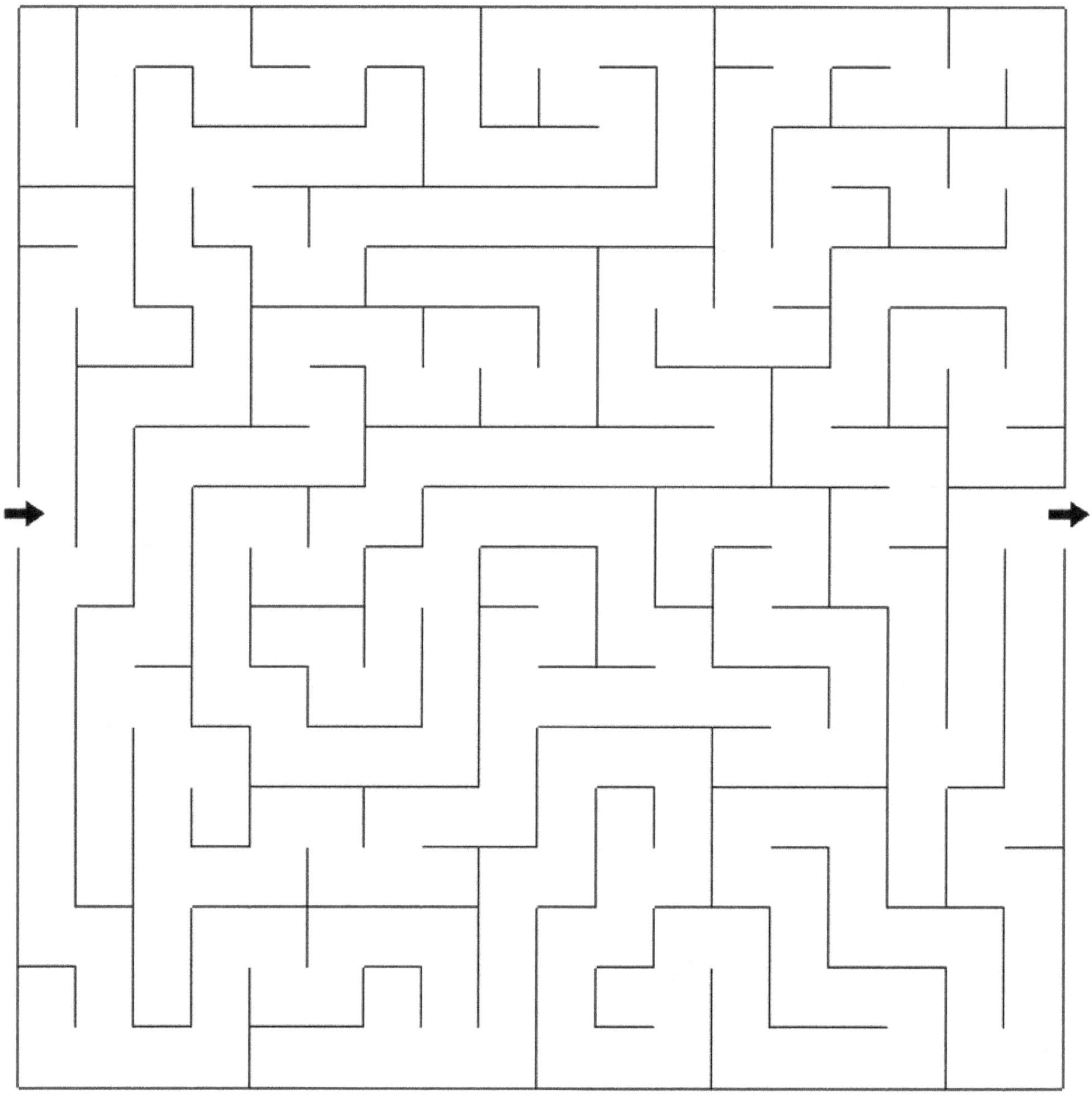

26

27

28

29

30

31

32

33

34

35

36

37

38

39

40

41

42

43

44

45

46

47

48

49

50

51

52

53

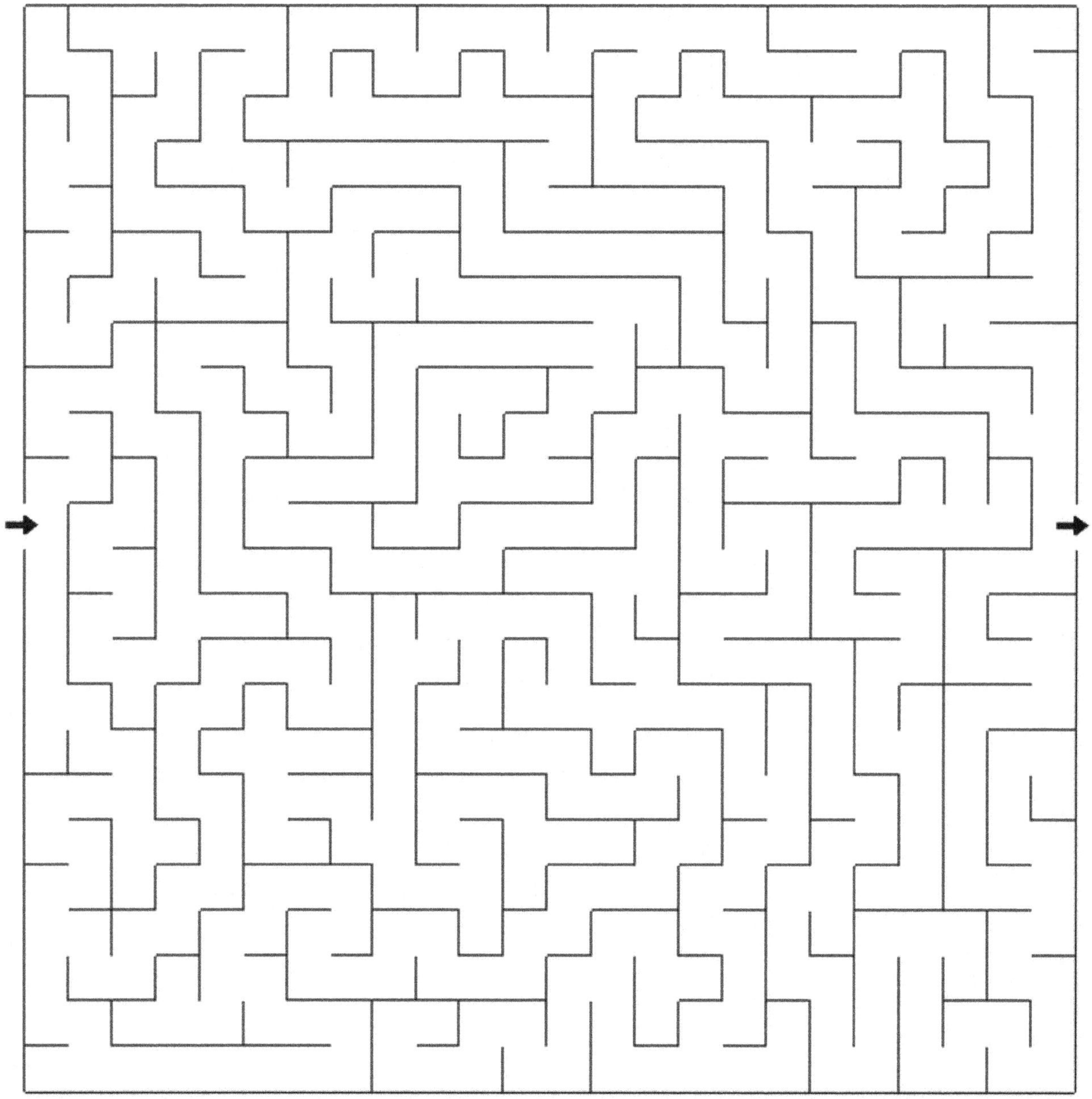

54

55

56

57

58

59

60

61

62

63

64

65

66

67

68

69

70

71

72

73

74

75

76

77

78

79

80

81

82

83

84

85

86

87

88

89

90

91

92

93

94

95

96

97

98

99

100

101

102

103

104

105

106

107

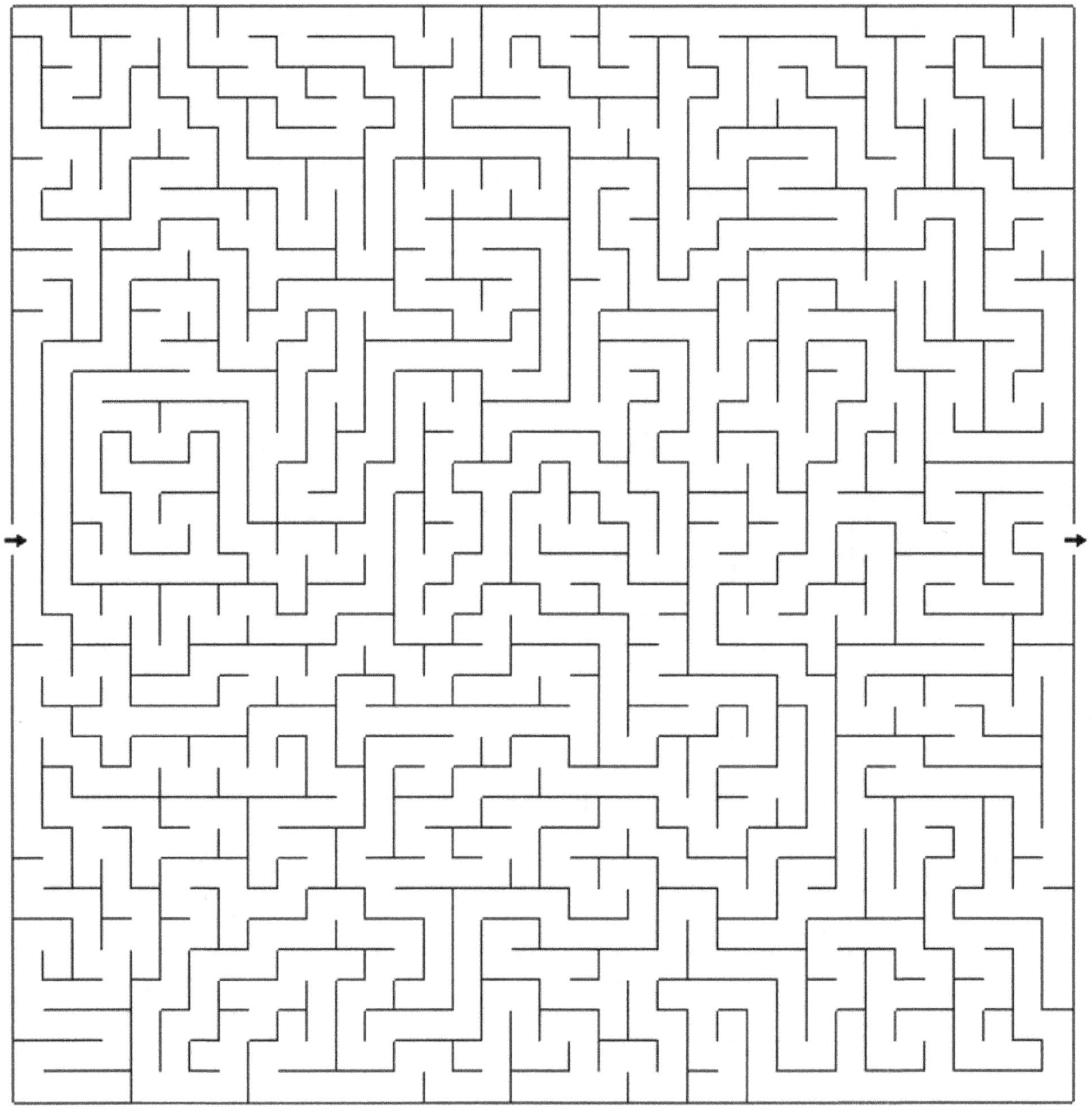

108

109

110

111

112

113

114

115

116

117

118

119

120

121

122

123

124

125

126

127

128

129

130

131

132

133

134

135

136

137

138

139

140

141

142

143

144

145

146

147

148

149

150

151

152

153

154

155

156

157

158

159

160

161

162

163

164

165

166

167

168

169

170

171

172

173

174

175

176

177

178

179

180

181

182

183

184

185

186

187

188

189

190

191

192

193

194

195

196

197

198

199

200

1

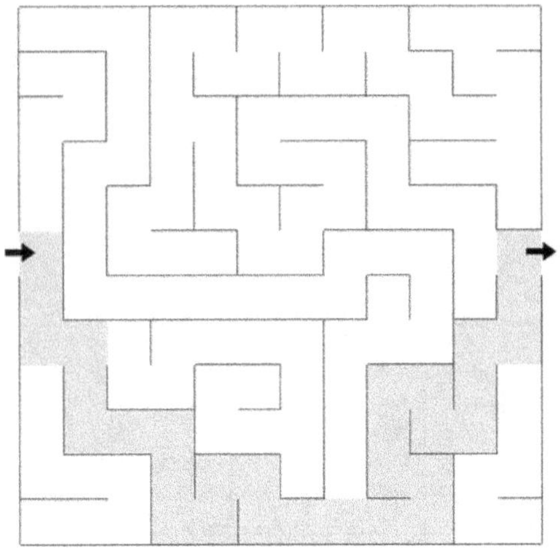

2

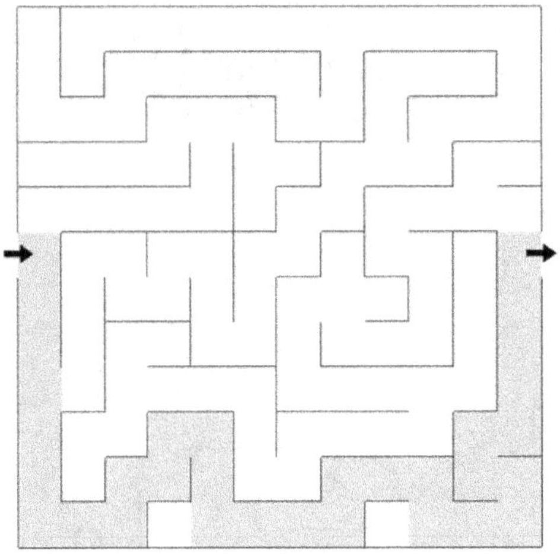

3

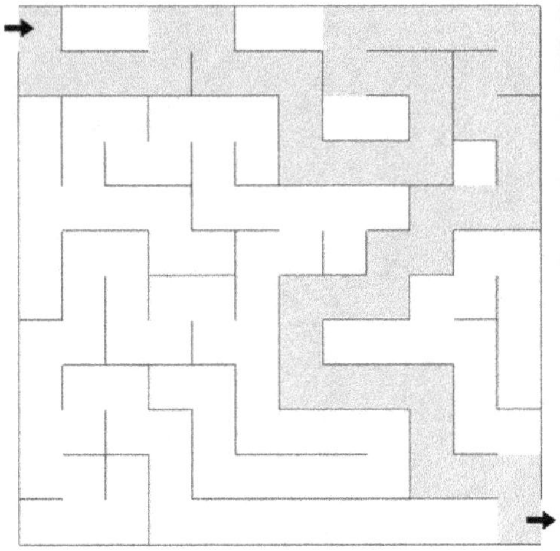

4

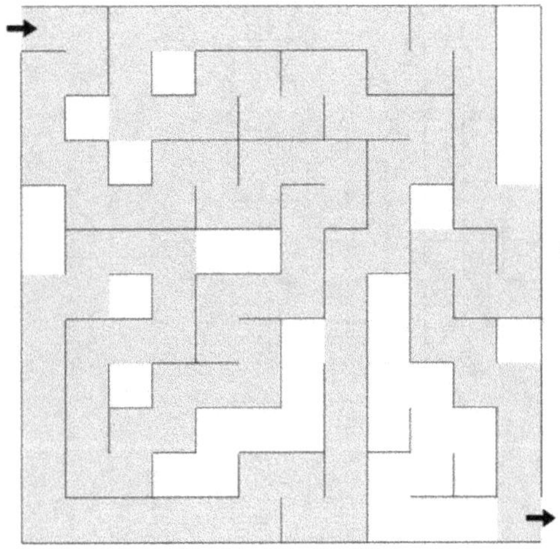

5

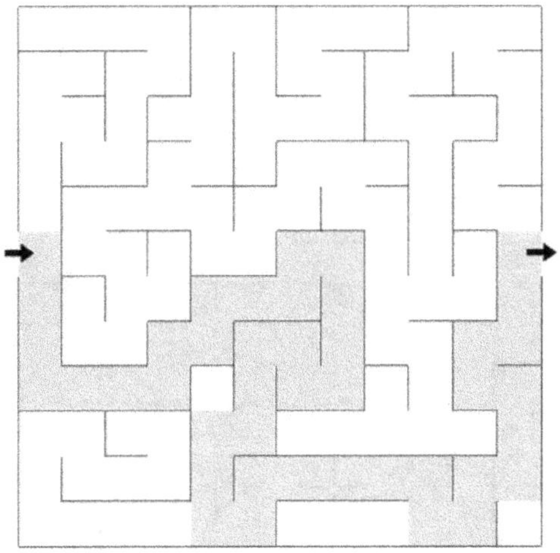

6

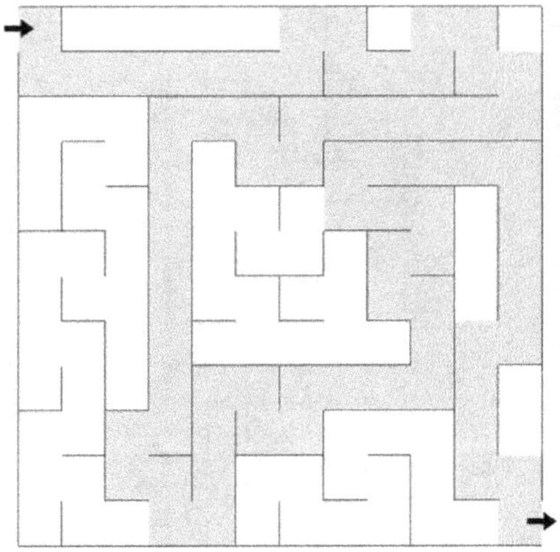

7

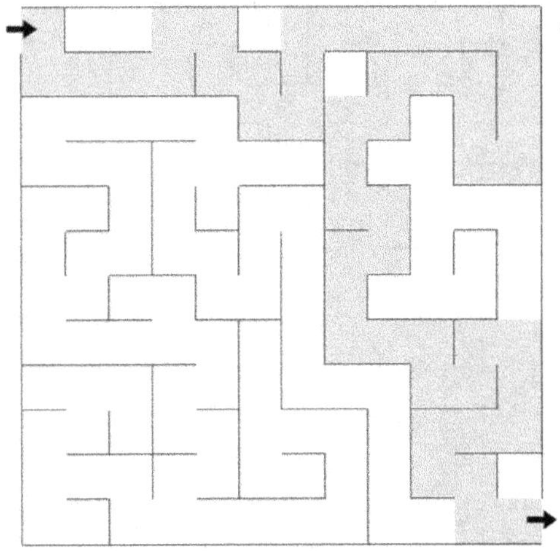

8

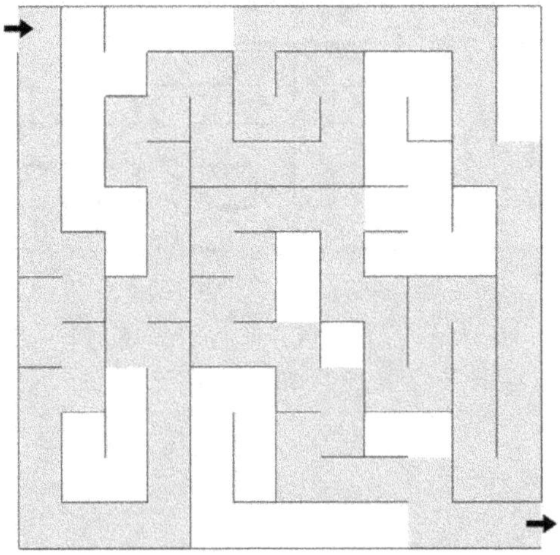

9

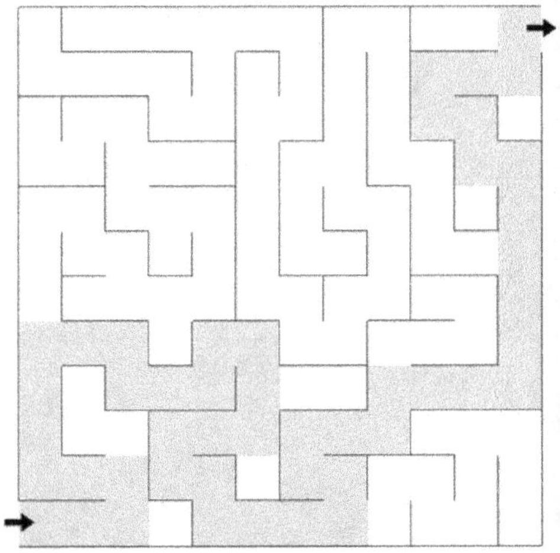

10

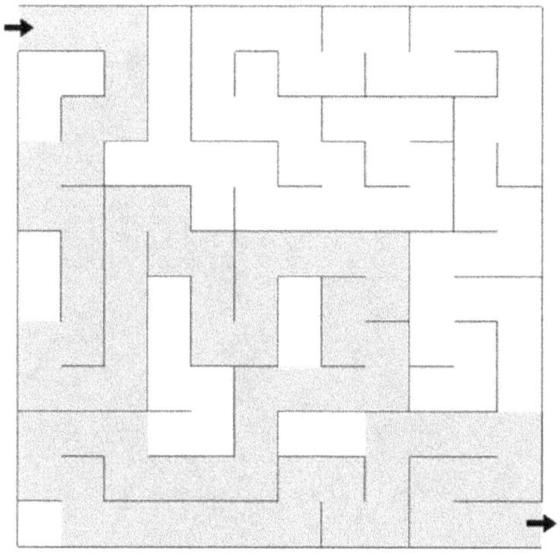

11

12

13

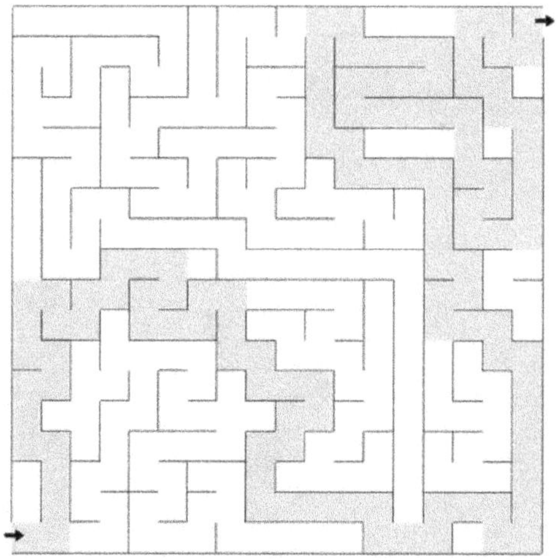

14

15

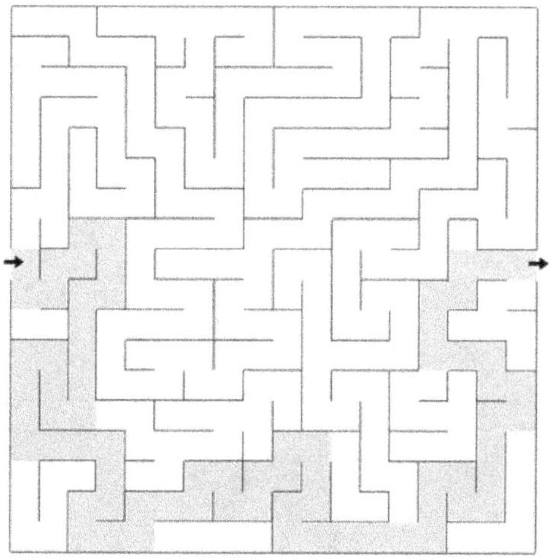

16

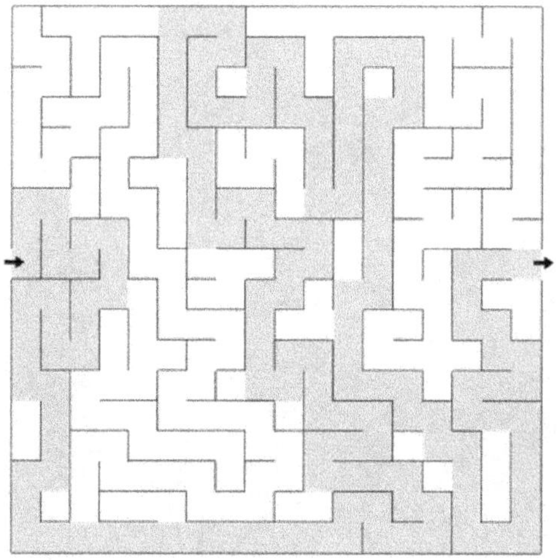

17

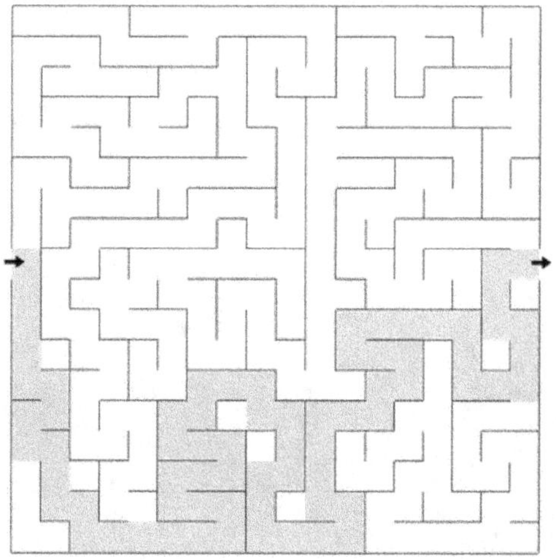

18

19

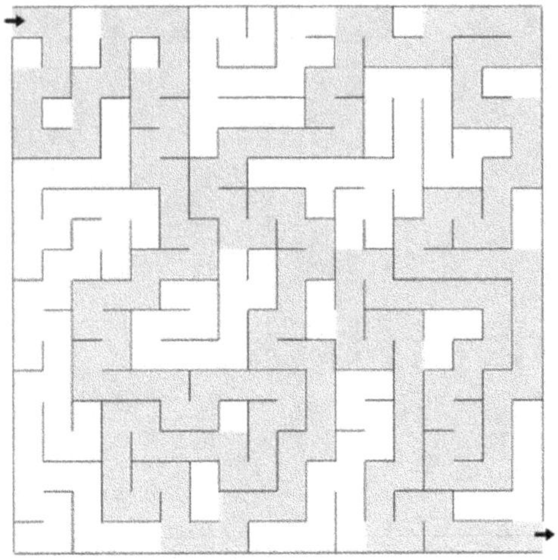

20

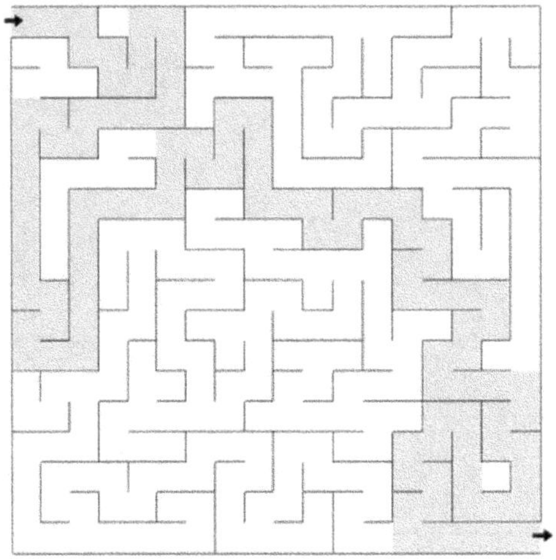

21

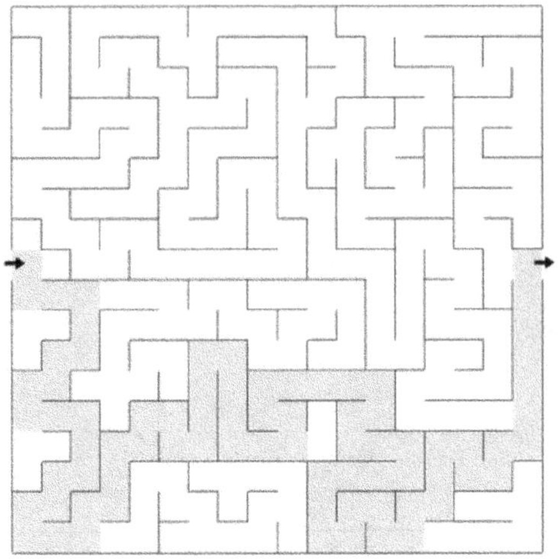

22

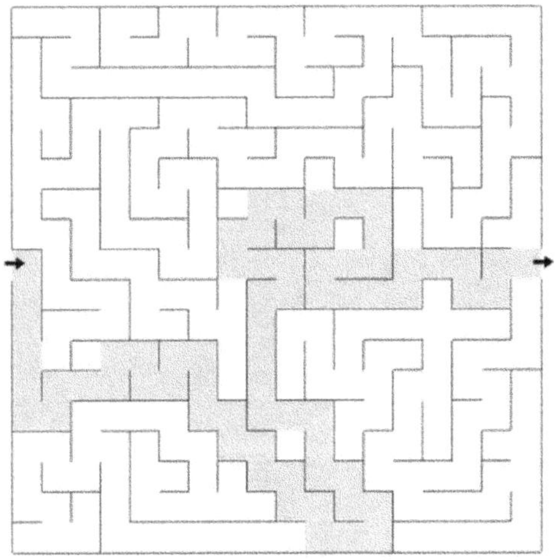

23

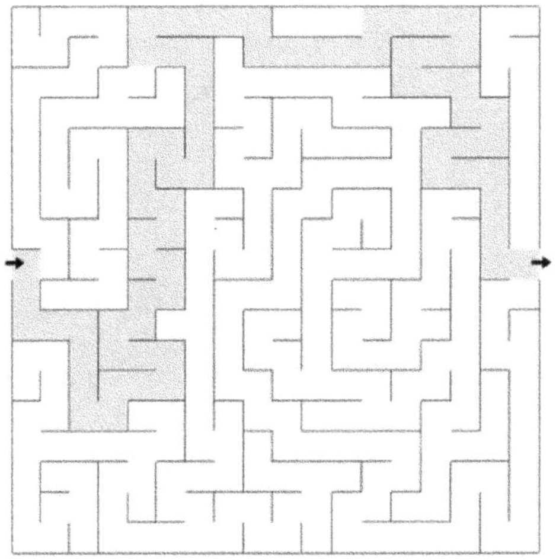

24

25

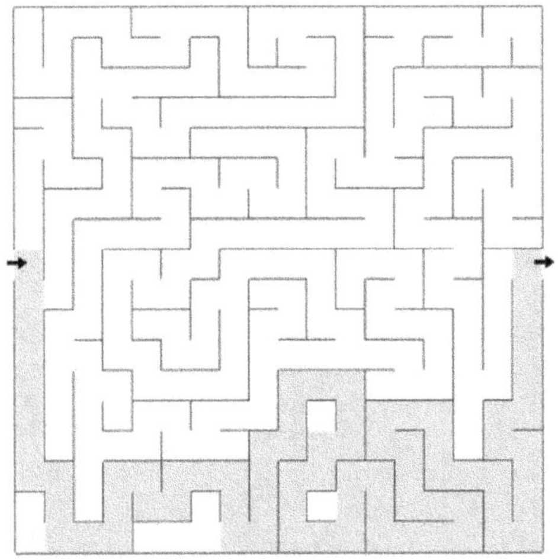

26

27

28

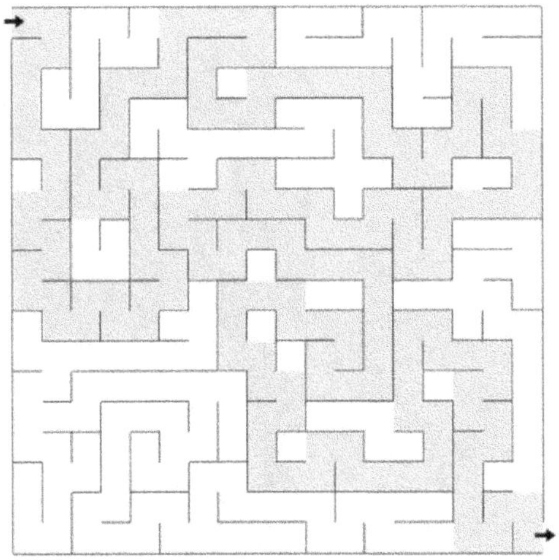

29

30

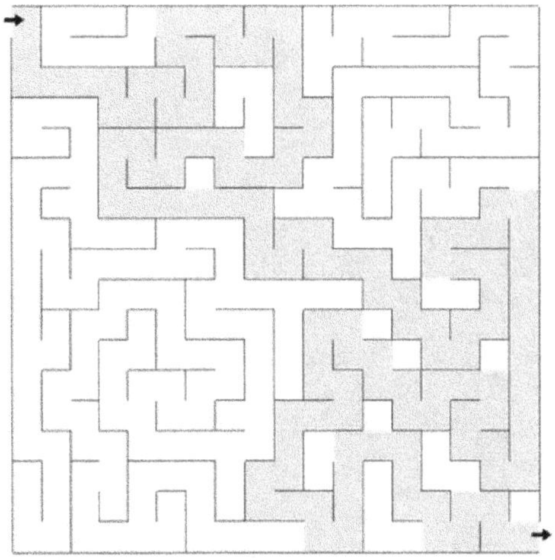

31

32

33

34

35

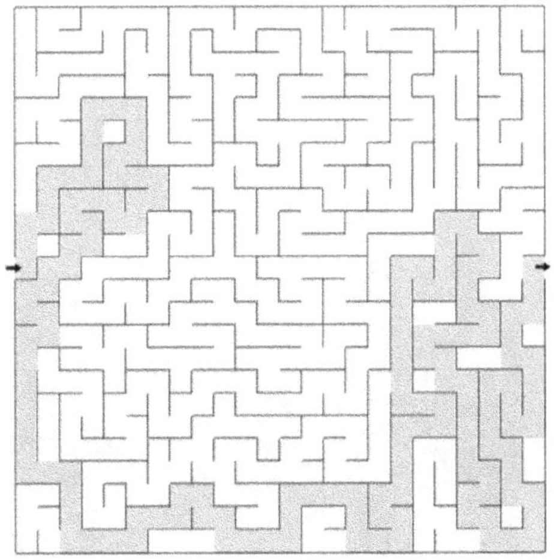

36

37

38

39

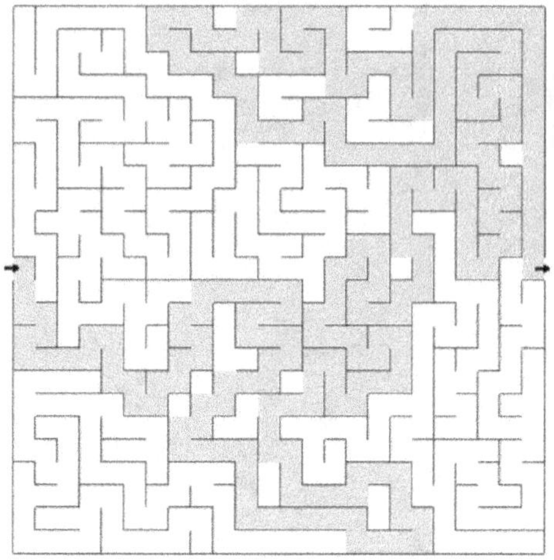

40

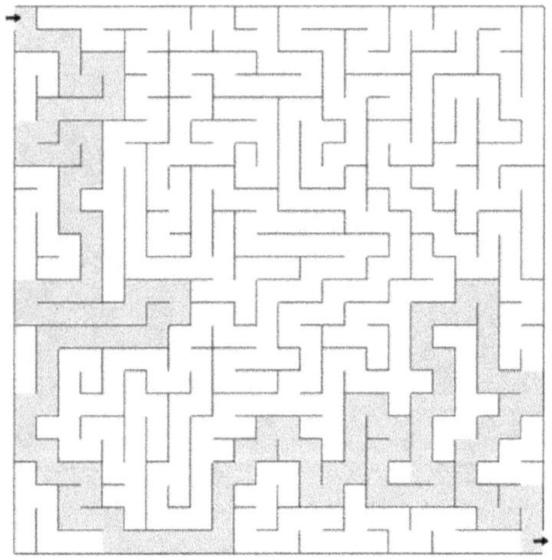

41

42

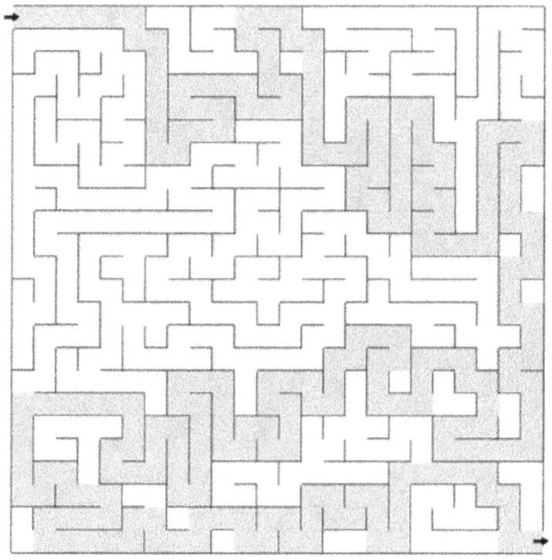

43

44

45

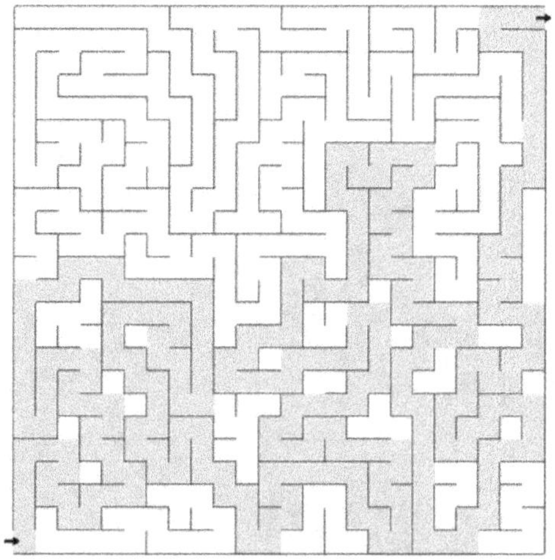

46

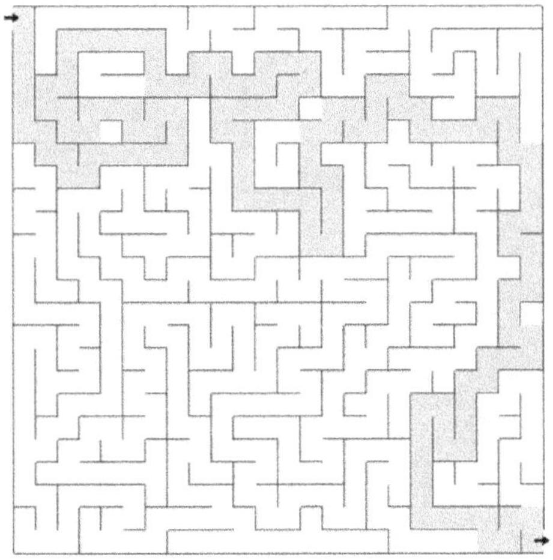

47

48

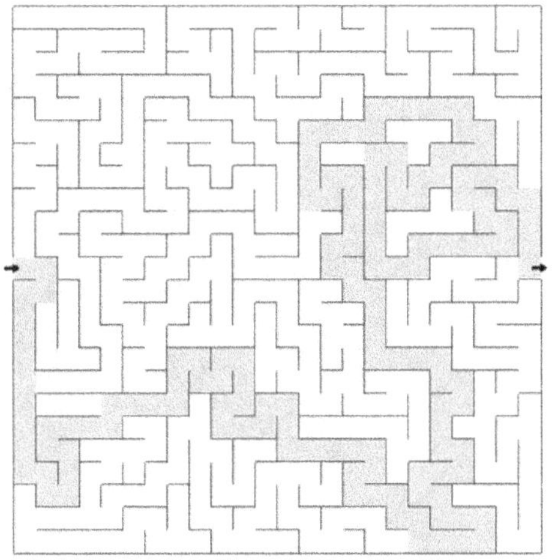

49

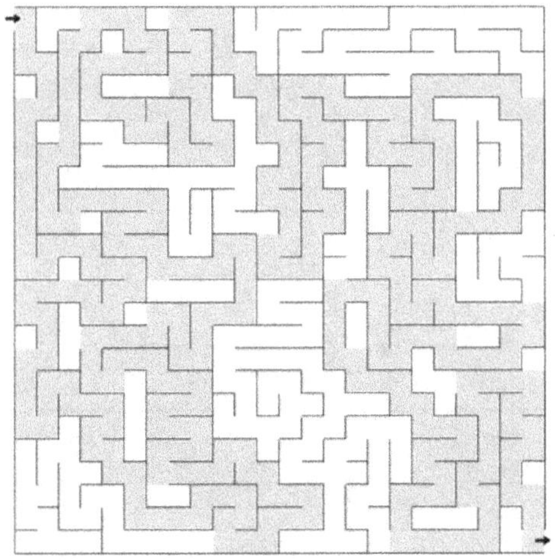

50

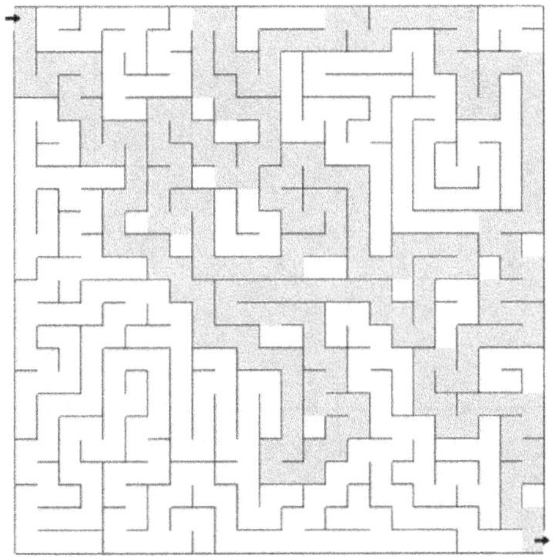

51

52

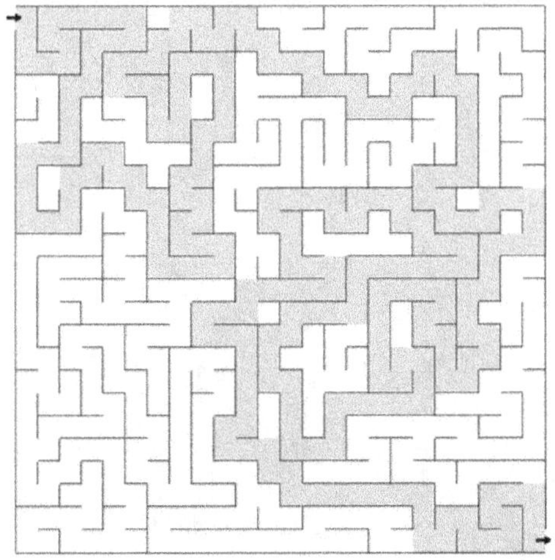

53

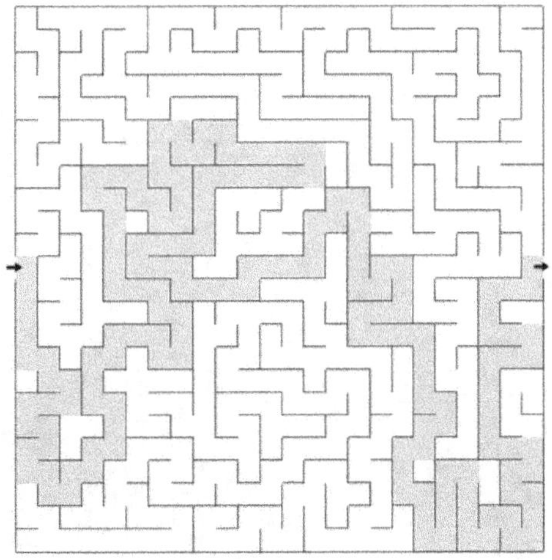

54

55

56

57

58

59

60

61

62

63

64

65

66

67

68

69

70

71

72

73

74

75

76

77

78

79

80

81

82

83

84

85

86

87

88

89

90

91

92

93

94

95

96

97

98

99

100

101

102

103

104

105

106

107

108

109

110

111

112

113

114

115

116

117

118

119

120

121

122

123

124

125

126

127

128

129

130

131

132

133

134

135

136

137

138

139

140

141

142

143

144

145

146

147

148

149

150

151

152

153

154

155

156

157

158

159

160

161

162

163

164

165

166

167

168

169

170

171

172

173

174

175

176

177

178

179

180

181

182

183

184

185

186

187

188

189

190

191

192

193

194

195

196

197

198

199

200

IF YOU ENJOYED THIS BOOK AT ALL IT WOULD MEAN THE WORLD TO US IF YOU COULD LEAVE A QUICK REVIEW! IT REALLY HELPS US OUT :)

THANK YOU IN ADVANCE

www.ingramcontent.com/pod-product-compliance
Lightning Source LLC
Chambersburg PA
CBHW081346080526
44588CB00016B/2396